# THE JOURNEY

21 DAYS IN HIS PRESENCE

Neither have I gone back from the commandment of his lips; I have esteemed the words of his mouth more than my necessary *food*.
*Job 23:12 (KJV)*

# THE JOURNEY
## 21 DAYS IN HIS PRESENCE

# BISHOP RICK AUGUST

PUBLISHED BY SUFFICIENT GRACE PUBLISHING

# THE JOURNEY:
## 21 DAYS IN HIS PRESENCE

For more information to obtain rights, contact

Sufficient Grace Publishing
P.O. Box 7808, D'Iberville, MS 39540
1-601-336-0727
Email: info@sufficientgracepublishing.com
www.sufficientgracepublishing.com
An Apostolic-Pentecostal ministry dedicated to
Literary Evangelism
ISBN: 0-9777360-9-1


First Printing, July 2015

# DEDICATION

I owe a debt of gratitude to so many people who have contributed greatly to whatever modicum of success I've enjoyed. My wife, Tammi, and my wonderful children and grandchildren; I'm nothing without you!

The greatest people on the planet (in my humble opinion), the members, past and present, of Greater Grace, Biloxi. You give me wings.

The late Mrs. Yvonne B. August (Mama) and Ruby Ina Woods (Granny); Your lessons and correction have served me well.

The Honorable Bishop Heron Johnson and the late Honorable Bishop John H. Shaw; Your commitment to ministry is my standard. I dedicate these pages in your honor.

All scripture is given by inspiration of God, and is profitable for doctrine, for reproof, for correction, for instruction in righteousness.
*2 Timothy 3:16 (KJV)*

# TABLE OF CONTENTS

# INTRODUCTION

If you're like me, the last thing you think you need is another devotional. While they have their place and serve a need, (and I may pen one in the future), there is a plethora of those out there. I receive a few daily on my phone that provide daily inspiration and insight that blesses my life.

The Journey is not intended to fit into that space. In my mind, it is a 21 day EXPERIENCE that is able to be relived repeatedly, with each encounter yielding its own unique fruit. I know people who travel to the same place every year on vacation. While the familiarity provides a framework for comfort, each year they return energized and refreshed as they relate some NEW experience they had on their journey.

Here are three recommendations that will maximize the impact of The Journey in your life.

1. **Document your experience**
   Write down your thoughts, emotions, as well as revelation, instructions, and insight you receive from the Lord. You may already keep a journal, but I recommend that you keep a separate one, so as to provide a frame of reference on future Journeys.

2. **Consecrate**
   During your Journey, set aside times of prayer and fasting that are above and beyond your normal private time with God.

Also, while total isolation is NOT necessary, seasons of sequestration are encouraged.

3. **Journey with others**
   The Journey works whether you take it alone or with others. From time to time, you may want to take it with others. This provides expanded insight as well as strength and accountability.

Well, off you go! May the Lord bless you on your Journey!

# DAY 1- THE JOURNEY
# THE WORD OF GOD

*Memory Verse: 2 Timothy 3:16*

*All scripture is given by inspiration of God, and is profitable for doctrine, for reproof, for correction, for instruction in righteousness.*

**Today's Scripture Reading:** Matthew 4:1-11, John 1

As Christians, we believe the Bible to be the infallible, inerrant, Word of God. The Scriptures declare that holy men wrote it under the inspiration of God (2 Peter 1:21). It is our compass (Psalm 119:105), our spiritual sustenance (Matthew 4:4), and our supreme authority (Psalm 138:2).

As such, we should have a DAILY RELATIONSHIP with the Word. After all, the Word is God (John 1:1). Our time with the Word should not be rushed or cursory. It should be planned, intimate, and given prime time in our day.

When a believer makes the Word of God, and obedience to the same, preeminent, he or she has an excellent foundation upon which to build Christian Character. Daily Bible reading cleanses us from the accumulated particles of carnality we gather through necessary interaction with those who are lost (John 15:3, John 17:17, Psalm 119:9).

Have you committed to a DAILY devotion to the Word of God?

**RECOMMENDATIONS:**

Commit to Reading the Bible EVERYDAY.
Make IT (the Word of God) the final authority in your life.
Carve out time to study regularly (2 Timothy 2:15).
As natural food is to our body, so is the Word of God to our spirit man; Eat, Eat, Eat (Job 23:12)!!!

*Memory Verse: Job 23:12*

*Neither have I gone back from the commandment of his lips; I have esteemed the words of his mouth more than my necessary food.*

*Journey Notes:*

# DAY 2 – THE JOURNEY
## PRAYER

*Memory Verse: Luke 18:1*

*And he spake a parable unto them to this end, that men ought always to pray, and not to faint.*

**Today's Scripture Reading:** Luke 18:1-8, John 2

Prayer has long been an area in which many believers have felt inadequate. The religious which represents prayer as arcane, coupled with the personal insecurities of Christians, have contributed to this phenomenon that has resulted in a prayer deficiency among the ranks of believers.

Prayer should not be intimidating. It is simply talking (making your requests known) to God (Philippians 4:6). There is no set volume, pitch, or rhythm with which the Scripture tells us to pray. One thing that is necessary for success in prayer is persistence.

In our Scripture reading today, the widow, whose means of support was gone, relies TOTALLY upon the unjust judge for relief. She does so because she realizes that he is THE ONLY one who can meet the need. She sets her face through repeated rejection. Because her cause was just and she would not give up, she received her deliverance.

If persistence and consistency (day and night) could yield such results in the court of an unjust judge, how much more in the court of The Righteous Judge (Luke 18:7)!

Will you make a commitment today to be persistent in prayer?

> *And shall not God avenge his own elect, which cry day and night unto him, though he bear long with them? Luke 18:7*

## RECOMMENDATIONS:

Set a time to pray. Don't compromise it.
Block out all distractions.
Be focused. Make a list, if necessary.
Take time to LISTEN for God's voice.
Be Spirit Led. There's no such thing as too much prayer.

*Journey Notes:*

# DAY 3- THE JOURNEY
## FASTING

*Memory Verse: Isaiah 58:5*

*Is it such a fast that I have chosen? a day for a man to afflict his soul? is it to bow down his head as a bulrush, and to spread sackcloth and ashes under him? wilt thou call this a fast, and an acceptable day to the LORD?*

**Today's Scripture Reading:** 1 Corinthians 9: 24-27, John 3

One of our greatest enemies, as believers, is the flesh. The Greek word for flesh is "sarx." It denotes mere human nature, the earthly nature of man apart from divine influence, and therefore prone to sin and opposed to God. How horrifying!!! To think that there is a part of each of us that cannot submit to God (Romans 8:7)! Our sin nature is incorrigible. There is no hope of redeeming it. It must be crucified (Galatians 5:24).

## AND THEY THAT ARE CHRIST'S HAVE CRUCIFIED THE FLESH WITH THE AFFECTIONS AND LUSTS.

One of the methodologies for crucifixion of the sin nature is prayer WITH FASTING. Fasting must ALWAYS be accompanied by prayer in order to yield spiritual results. It should also be accompanied by acts of service (Isaiah 58:7).

*Is it not to deal thy bread to the hungry, and that thou bring the poor that are cast out to thy house? when thou seest the naked, that thou cover him; and that thou hide not thyself from thine own flesh?*

Many people believe fasting to be antiquated, but Jesus specifically pointed forward to our day when He said "then shall they fast." Fasting means "not to eat." Abstaining from the consumption of food, combined with avoiding pleasurable activities, buffets the body of sin by keeping it under subjection to the Holy Spirit (Isaiah 58:3, 1 Corinthians 7:5, Romans 6:6, 1 Corinthians 9:27).

## Three Types of Fasts

1. Normal – Water Only up to 30 days
2. Absolute- No food or water up to 3 days
3. Partial – No pleasant (processed) foods without a time limit

## Additional Scriptures:

*Psalm 35:13 - But as for me, when they were sick, my clothing was sackcloth: I humbled my soul with fasting; and my prayer returned into mine own bosom.*

*Psalm 69:10 - When I wept, and chastened my soul with fasting, that was to my reproach.*

*Psalm 109:24 - My knees are weak through fasting; and my flesh faileth of fatness.*

*Daniel 6:18 - Then the king went to his palace, and passed the night fasting: neither were instruments of musick brought before him: and his sleep went from him.*

*Matthew 17:21- Howbeit this kind goeth not out but by prayer and fasting.*

Are you willing to (begin, maintain, have, commit to, etc) regular seasons of fasting?

## RECOMMENDATIONS:

Don't look like you're fasting (Matt 6:17).

Replace your designated eating time with the Word, prayer, and service to others.

Avoid distractions (television, newspaper, telephone, computer, carnal conversations, etc.).

*Journey Notes:*

*Journey Notes:*

# DAY 4 – THE JOURNEY
# THE VOICE OF GOD

*Memory Verse: Proverbs 3:5-6*

*Trust in the LORD with all thine heart; and lean not unto thine own understanding. In all thy ways acknowledge him, and he shall direct thy paths.*

**Today's Scripture Reading:** John 10:1-30, John 4

From the beginning of time, God has fostered a relationship with us through His voice. Adam, the first man, communed with a God he never saw but heard (John 1:18, Genesis 3:8). Through God's voice, Adam received instruction, direction, and correction. God's methodology for communication with man has not changed. Satan is keenly aware of this fact and is constantly attempting to obfuscate God's voice. It is God's will that we KNOW His voice.

God is a God of precedent. The "Logos" (written Word) is the foundation and proving ground for the "Rhema" (uttered Word). God speaks to us through His Word, His Spirit, His preacher, as well as through other people. God is able to use anything created to communicate with us (Colossians 1:20). Through DAILY Scripture reading, we become familiar with the character and nuances of God's voice. Just as in our personal relationships, we know a person's speech pattern and vocabulary; so it is in the realm of the Spirit.

In our Scripture reading today, Jesus makes four allusions to His sheep (us), either hearing or knowing His voice. We are not to "believe every spirit" rather, we are to "try" (test) them by the Word of God (1 John 4:1).

## RECOMMENDATIONS:

Make it a habit to confirm every voice by the Word of God. Spend inordinate amounts of time in the Word of God familiarizing yourself with His character.

Reject any voice that does not line up TOTALLY with God's character and the established nuances of His voice.

*Journey Notes:*

# DAY 5 – THE JOURNEY
## TIME APART

*Memory Verse: Mark 6:31*

*And he said unto them, Come ye yourselves apart into a desert place, and rest a while: for there were many coming and going, and they had no leisure so much as to eat.*

**Today's Scripture Reading:** Mark 1:28-35; John 5

The hustle and bustle of everyday life allows for little private or alone time. It might surprise you to know how little time you actually spend not being bombarded by commercials, demands, requests, requirements, and deadlines. God Himself set the tone when on the seventh day He rested (ceased from labor) (Genesis 2:2-3).

I believe that there are three types of rest:

1. Spiritual-the SOUL that is free from the penalty of sin (Matt 11:28).
2. Physical-the BODY that is free from labor (Mark 6:31).
3. Mental-the MIND that is free from worry (Philippians 4:6).

Rest is a command from God, and should be scheduled (Exodus 23:12). Jesus made a habit of separating himself from the press, rabble, and crowds that thronged Him all wanting something from Him. He lovingly and compassionately met their needs, but was sensitive to His own need for spiritual, physical, and mental replenishment.

Rest recharges the battery, recovers strength, and restores mental agility. If you would be all that God ordained, plan seasons of rest. Not to be confused with a vacation, rest may be accomplished at home. It need not be long to yield the necessary results. The one prerequisite is that YOU MUST BE ALONE!!! This is not "ME" time. This is time alone with God! You'll be amazed at what 8-24 hours of REAL REST would accomplish.

## RECOMMENDATIONS:

Dis-Connect – Step away from all noise: television, radio, telephone, people, and problems.

Dis-Engage – Be sure that your mind is not preoccupied with any thoughts that would cause it to exert itself.

Dis-Cover – Expect to see, hear, and experience things heretofore unknown.

*Be sure to set a Start and Stop time. This will prevent procrastination going in and coming out.

*Journey Notes:*

# DAY 6 – THE JOURNEY
## WORSHIP

*Memory Verse: John 4:23-24*

*But the hour cometh, and now is, when the true worshippers shall worship the Father in spirit and in truth: for the Father seeketh such to worship him. God is a Spirit: and they that worship him must worship him in spirit and in truth.*

**Today's Scripture Reading:** Isaiah 6:1-8, John 6

Two terms heard regularly among believers are "praise" and "worship." While the object of the affection of both of them is the same, Jesus, the motivation differs. Praise is purely experiential, while worship is revelational as well as experiential. Praise is usually an expression of gratitude for someTHING God has done, while worship is an act of reverence based upon the revelation of WHO God is.

In our scripture reading today, Isaiah recounts his "seeing" the Lord. God allows Isaiah to behold His Holiness. In awe, he humbles himself in the presence of God and has a life-altering experience. The Greek word for worship is "proskyneo," meaning to kiss the hand, to fall upon the knees and touch the ground with the forehead as an expression of reverence. There are degrees of worship which are commensurate with the degree of revelation of God to the individual. It follows then that all worship is not the same (Mark 5:1-5). It is possible to have an encounter with Jesus, or even be a follower of His, and not have a supernatural revelation of His character and nature (Acts 9:1-5, Matt 16:13-17).

Because God's nature is infinite, there are infinite dimensions of worship. Whenever God reveals some facet of His nature, it will result in a simultaneous revelation of our deficiency in that same aspect of our nature. This should trigger what I call The Worship Cycle.

## THE WORSHIP CYCLE

**Revelation** - God unveils some aspect of His nature to an individual.
**Response Primitus** (first) - Humility, gratitude, and repentance on the part of said individual.
**Result** - Cleansing of said individual for service.
**Royal Solicitation** - A call from the King for individual service on behalf of the realm.
**Response Secundus** (second) - Said individual answers the call of duty with zeal and vigor.

## RECOMMENDATIONS:

Wait regularly on the Lord until He chooses to reveal Himself to you on some level.
Take prompt and deliberate action in response to the revelation (Honor God, humble yourself).
Listen for the call of duty.

*Journey Notes:*

# DAY 7 – THE JOURNEY
# FAITHFULNESS

*Memory Verse: 1 Corinthians 4:2*

*Moreover it is required in stewards, that a man be
found faithful.*

**Today's Scripture Reading:** Luke 12:31-48, John 7

Normally, when we hear the term faithfulness, it's either associated with marriage or money. In truth, faithfulness is applicable to every part of our lives. Webster defines faithfulness as the quality of being loyal, constant, and steadfast. These attributes are often aspired to in secular endeavors, but often times in spiritual conquests, a lackluster approach suffices.

In Kingdom affairs, we should exhibit faithfulness because He who called us is faithful in all things (1 Corinthians 1:9, Lamentations 3:23, James 1:17). Trust, consistency, timeliness, and commitment are the four elements of faithfulness. As stewards (managers) of God's resources, we should always be willing to give of the time, talents, and treasure with which we've been entrusted. We are His disciples, which infers that we are to lead disciplined lives. Years ago, someone shared with me this definition of discipline: Doing WHAT you know you should do, WHEN you know you should do it, THE WAY you know you should do it, even when you don't FEEL like it, without anybody

TELLING YOU to do it. Are you a feelings person? If so, faithfulness will be a challenge for you as will success because the two go hand in hand (Joshua 1:8).

> *This book of the law shall not depart out of thy mouth; but thou shalt meditate therein day and night, that thou mayest observe to do according to all that is written therein: for then thou shalt make thy way prosperous, and then thou shalt have good success. (Joshua 1:8)*

Faithfulness cannot be selective. By definition, it cannot be. What we are in the least, we will be in the greatest. What we are with little, we will be with much. Jesus said that He must be about His Father's "business." He also said that we should occupy until He came.

## RECOMMENDATIONS:

### Take the Faithfulness Quiz:

1. Can you be trusted to fulfill assignments, even under pressure?
2. Are you consistent in your obedience to God's voice, even when it's hard?
3. Do you operate in a punctual manner in the things of God?
4. Are you reliable and dependable in spiritual matters, or do you require constant reminders, motivation, or correction to prompt you to action?

*Journey Notes:*

# DAY 8 – THE JOURNEY
## THE PRESENCE OF THE LORD

*Memory Verse: Psalm 16:11*

*Thou wilt shew me the path of life: in thy presence is fulness of joy; at thy right hand there are pleasures for evermore.*

**Today's Scripture Reading:** 1 Kings 8:5-11, John 8

The subject of God's presence is inexhaustible, but over the next few days, Lord willing, we want to delve into the meaning, significance, and attainment of His presence. In today's Scripture text, God's glory filled the house of the Lord. His presence was so prominent that the priests could not exercise their normal duties of ministry. The Greek word Kabowd intimates that the presence of God has weight, splendor, and dignity to it.

We understand that God is omnipresent (everywhere present simultaneously), but for purposes of this discourse, let's just say that His presence is more prominently displayed in some places than others. This is significant because there are things that can occur in His presence that absolutely CANNOT occur outside of His presence.

Where God is worshipped, He will make His presence manifest. The degree of manifestation is proportional to the level of worship. You may remember from a previous lesson that the level of worship is connected to the level of revelation. So then, the process is flow: Revelation, Worship, and Manifestation.

It is significant that this overwhelming display of God's presence was preceded by an overwhelming display of sacrificial worship on the part of King Solomon and all the congregation of Israel (1 Kings 8:5). Notice that the glory follows the worship. It is in fact God's response to worship. Take the limits off of your worship. Don't measure it, but POUR IT OUT on God. His response will astound you!

*And king Solomon, and all the congregation of Israel, that*
*were assembled unto him, were with him before the ark,*
*sacrificing sheep and oxen, that could not be told nor numbered*
*for multitude. (1 Kings 8:5)*

## RECOMMENDATION:

Start sensing opportunities to go deeper into worship than you've previously gone.
Make sacrifices that honor God on a greater level.
Surround yourself with people who are similarly minded.

*Journey Notes:*

# DAY 9 – THE JOURNEY
# POWER IN HIS PRESENCE

*Memory Verse: 1 Chronicles 29:11*

*Thine, O LORD, is the greatness, and the power, and the glory, and the victory, and the majesty: for all that is in the heaven and in the earth is thine; thine is the kingdom, O LORD, and thou art exalted as head above all.*

**Today's Scripture Reading:** Luke 7:11-16, John 9

There are great and significant benefits to be enjoyed by those who dare to make a life of worship their priority. In the previous lesson, we highlighted the omnipresence of God. His omnipotence (all-powerfulness) always accompanies His presence. Wherever God is, His energy to do work is available. This power is unlimited in its depth and breadth. This means that there is nothing it cannot do and no place it cannot reach!

It is the Spirit of God that does the work (Zechariah 4:6). Every miracle that Jesus performed was by the Spirit that dwelled in Him. There was nothing supernatural about His flesh (Colossians 2:8-9). In the gospels, Jesus' flesh allowed us to locate and identify God's presence. Every miracle that happened when He showed up is a reminder of what is possible through the work of the invisible Spirit which indwells us (Ephesians 3:20).

The works that He did, we can, and WILL do (John 14:12)! By virtue of being filled with the Spirit, we are made conquerors over the flesh (Galatians 5:16). Remember, time in His presence is transformative. Attitudes, dispositions, and tendencies are all shaped in His presence. Live in the Spirit so you can walk in the Spirit (Galatians 5:25)!

> *Then he answered and spake unto me, saying, This is the word of the LORD unto Zerubbabel, saying, Not by might, nor by power, but by my spirit, saith the LORD of hosts.*
> *(Zechariah 4:6)*

## RECOMMENDATIONS:

Expect the demonstration of God's power:

To heal.
To deliver.
To save.
To transform.

*Journey Notes:*

# DAY 10 – THE JOURNEY
## PEACE IN HIS PRESENCE

*Memory Verse: John 14:27*

*Peace I leave with you, my peace I give unto you: not as the world giveth, give I unto you. Let not your heart be troubled, neither let it be afraid.*

**Today's Scripture Reading:** Mark 4:37-41; John 10

DON'T FALL FOR IT! Refuse to accept the pseudo-peace which is the world's cheap imitation of the authentic peace that God's presence guarantees. Tranquility, calm, restfulness, and quiet all sound good. These are all synonymous with the term peace, and under ordinary circumstances, we might gladly settle for them. But these are not ordinary times! To quote Founding Father Thomas Paine, "These are the times that try men's souls." The Apostle Paul looked prophetically through time and called these "perilous times."

This is exactly the reason that you and I cannot afford to accept a peace that has not been tested and approved. As in today's reading, like the disciples, we are sure to encounter stormy weather on life's journey. Tranquility and calm that have as their basis: intellect, connections, resources, and physical strength, will certainly dissipate under the barometric pressure associated with the storms that are sure to come in our lives (1 Peter 4:12).

Jesus tells us that His peace is not like the peace the world gives. The world's peace has a breaking point, which after it has been attained, is supplanted by fear and dread. The disciple's reaction was perfectly understandable. They had done well. They did all they could do and didn't wake Jesus until the boat was full of water! That's what lets us know that it wasn't perfect peace (Isaiah 26:3). Perfect peace, which is dependent upon His presence, is NOT understandable to the human mind. Neither you, nor the people who witness the severity of your storm, will be able to believe your calm, measured, and confident response (Philippians 4:7). This is because it comes from His strength, not yours. Are you enjoying the inexplicable peace that can only come from a life in God's presence?

## RECOMMENDATIONS:

Look for signs of God's peace in little storms.
Remember Who is in your ship when the winds begin to howl.
Speak to the winds and remind them of Who is in your vessel.

*Journey Notes:*

# DAY 11 – THE JOURNEY
## JOY IN HIS PRESENCE

*Memory Verse: Isaiah 12:3*

*Therefore with joy shall ye draw water out of the
wells of salvation.*

**Today' Scripture Reading:** I Chronicles 15:14-28, John 11

As we entertain the presence of the Lord, these "byproducts" of worship: power, peace, and now joy will flood our lives. For many years, I mistakenly pursued power, prayed for peace, and even leaped, literally, for joy. It was a classic case of pursuing the blessing instead of the Blesser. Joy is so pivotal in the life of the believer. God wants our lives to be full of joy (John 15:11, 16:24).

Peace and joy have a symbiotic relationship, kind of like red beans and rice. They appear together in scripture regularly. God wants us to enjoy our relationship with Him. It should not be laborious and tedious. Like all good relationships, it will require time, energy, and effort. But oh, the joy (Romans 14:7, 15:3)! The joy of the Lord strengthens and refreshes us (Nehemiah 8:10). Of course, there are duties and responsibilities associated with serving the Lord, but even these are tempered by the Joy of the Lord.

As King David and those who accompanied him, brought the Ark of the Covenant back to its rightful place, there was great joy! The ark represented the presence of the Lord. When God's presence is the preeminent desire in our lives, then we will hunger and thirst for intimacy with Him (Psalms 42:1, 2); when we live to worship Him; THEN will our lives be filled with a cascading, exhilarating, triumphant, jubilation of Joy!

## RECOMMENDATIONS:

Evaluate your Joy to Duty ratio.
Linger longer in His presence.
Count your blessings, not your problems.

*Journey Notes:*

# DAY 12 – THE JOURNEY
## POSITIVE CONFESSION

*Memory Verse: James 3:10*

*Out of the same mouth proceedeth blessing and cursing.*
*My brethren, these things ought not so to be.*

**Today's Scripture Reading:** Genesis 1, John 12

Words are powerful! All that we see was created by the Word of God (Hebrews 11:3). And God said... is a redundant theme in creation. Words have creative power with the capacity to produce life or death (Proverbs 18:21). Our words produce consequences whether we intend them to or not (Proverbs 6:2).

Knowing this, we should ensure that our words are positive, faith-filled, and life-giving. Don't speak idle words which are words that aren't positively charged (Matthew 12:36, Ephesians 4:29). Speaking should be a process. Think before you speak. Evaluate the weight of your words and decide whether to utter them. If they are negatively charged, don't say them. If they are positively charged, utter them as succinctly as possible. This is applicable in our relationship with God as well (Ecclesiastes 5:2, 6).

We are not reporters who have a mandate to tell what we see or feel in the natural. As the seed of Abraham, we have the God-given right to declare a thing that is not, as though it were. We say a thing that is not so, as though it were so, until it becomes so (Romans 4:17)! We do not confess the negative, we proclaim the positive (Joel 3:10)! This will yield a bountiful harvest of blessings and favor in our lives.

## RECOMMENDATIONS:

Monitor your words: are they few, positive, and faith-filled?
Listen more, talk less.
Use your words to uplift others.

*Journey Notes:*

# DAY 13 – THE JOURNEY
## POSITIVE MEDITATION

*Memory Verse: Psalm 19:14*

*Let the words of my mouth, and the meditation of my heart, be
acceptable in thy sight, O LORD, my strength, and
my redeemer.*

**Today's Scripture Reading:** Philippians 4:8, John 13

We've established the importance of words as creative forces in the earth. This would lead to the natural conclusion that if we desire to walk in the fullness of God's plan for us, we should focus the bulk of our attention on changing our speech patterns. To that I say, Yes AND No. In a way, words are the manifested fruit of our thoughts which originate, or are incubated in our minds (Luke 6:45).

Believe it or not, we have the capacity to control our thought life. We can generate, reject, receive, and retrieve thoughts. If the preponderance of our focus is on making sure that our seeds (thoughts) are positive and productive then fruit (words) will automatically be the same. In every word (fruit) are many seeds with the potential to yield a GREAT harvest. Mahatma Gandhi has said, "Your beliefs become your thoughts, your thoughts become your words, your words become your actions, your actions become your habits, your habits become your values, your values become your destiny."

Don't water negative seeds! Don't allow others to plant ungodly seeds in the garden of your mind. Put a fence around your mind. Guard, cleanse, and cultivate it (Proverbs 4:23). Read hortative literature, engage in edifying conversation, and fill your heart (mind) with the Word of God. It's tempting to overlook our thought life because it's invisible, but remember, it's only a matter of time before our words and actions reveal our thoughts. Great thoughts, Great words, Great life!

## RECOMMENDATIONS:

Examine your thought life.
Weed the garden of your mind.
Evaluate what you are placing in your heart.

*Journey Notes:*

# DAY 14 – THE JOURNEY
## REPENTANCE

*Memory Verse: 2 Chronicles 7:14*

*If my people, which are called by my name, shall humble themselves, and pray, and seek my face, and turn from their wicked ways; then will I hear from heaven, and will forgive their sin, and will heal their land.*

**Today's Scripture Reading:** 2 Samuel 11 & 12, John 14

A change of mind that results in changed behavior is my simplistic definition of repentance. A strong differentiation should be made between behavior modification and true repentance. Behavior modification is a psychological response to undesirable behavior. It is outside-in change that requires triggers, boundaries, and consequences for success. Repentance is inside-out change that conditions the heart and modifies the desire. Repentance requires an acknowledgement of sin (transgression against God's Word), confession (an expression of responsibility and regret, accompanied by a desire to change), and turning (physical and spiritual activity that is the evidence of a changed heart).

As we interact with God, He invariably will reveal to us areas of deficit in our lives. As in the case with David, when he was confronted with his sin, our response should be one of humility and contrition. Our cry should be, "Create in me a clean heart O God"

(Psalm 51:10). Repentance is a key to growth and refreshing. During the balance of David's life, we find no record of him EVER repeating this egregious act. Repentance prevents repetition of sinful acts.

Sin blocks our line of communication with God (Isaiah 59:1-2). No acts of kindness or service can substitute for repentance. Genuine praise is hindered and authentic worship is impossible when we operate in sin. The good news is that God will restore, renew, and revive if we repent. We should constantly ask God to search us. We should not attempt to search our own hearts because we aren't qualified to perform such a formidable task (Psalm 139:23, Jeremiah 17:9). This constant purging will keep a freshness in our relationship with the Savior as we journey.

## RECOMMENDATIONS:

Submit your heart to the Lord, Jesus, for spiritual inspection.
When areas of disobedience are revealed, repent quickly.
Live an inside-out life.

*Journey Notes:*

# DAY 15 – THE JOURNEY
## ACCOUNTABILITY

*Memory Verse: Romans 14:12*

*So then every one of us shall give account of himself to God.*

**Today's Scripture Reading:** Matthew 25:14-29, John 15

In a previous lesson, we discussed the subject of faithfulness. Closely associated with faithfulness is the characteristic of accountability. Faithfulness addresses the what, when, where, and how of our walk with God. Accountability focuses on the why. Responsibility and a ready answer are both aspects of accountability.

Each of us has been given gifts and callings that differ according to our individual ability. It is our responsibility to cover, cultivate, and maximize the potential of that gifting. God's expectation is that there be a return on His investment which is commensurate in proportionality to the gift (Luke 12:48). If you and I would ever be greatly used of God, we must eliminate the practice blame shifting, excuse making, and shoulder shrugging. We must be actively engaged in a plan to develop what has been entrusted to us. Jesus left instructions that we occupy until He comes (Luke 19:12, 13). We must take the initiative to advance God's Kingdom agenda in the earth.

When we are accountable, the motivation and inspiration comes from within. Reminders, rewards, and pep talks are not standard fare for us nor is perpetual correction and reproof. We are able to give a positive accounting of the resources under our authority and are ever mindful of that day of reckoning in eternity when we will give a final report of our stewardship. Every decision we make is made with this in mind. This allows us to give every man an answer when they ask a reason of the hope that is in us (1 Peter 3:15).

## RECOMMENDATIONS:

Take stock of the gifts you've been given by God. Be careful not to minimize ANY gift.
Ask yourself how you're using what you've been given to glorify God.
Evaluate the source of your spiritual motivation. Is it internal or external?

*Journey Notes:*

# DAY 16 – THE JOURNEY
## INTEGRITY

*Memory Verse: Proverbs 20:7*

*The just man walketh in his integrity: his children are blessed after him.*

**Today's Scripture Reading:** Job 2:1-9, John 16

In a world full of so many voices, where we're bombarded with a plethora of choices, it's important to be able to navigate through this maze we call life. To be sure that we don't "get lost" we must find our "true north" which is a fixed point that doesn't change. This point serves as a reference point for every other destination in our lives. For us as believers, the Word of God and the Spirit of God are our true north. Publicly, and privately, we move in syncopation with the will of God for us as directed by the Holy Ghost.

Our commitment to true north is called integrity. Integrity is the opposite of hypocrisy, in that it involves regarding INTERNAL consistency as a virtue. The word integrity is derived from the word integer which means whole or complete. The intimation is that people of integrity are not duplicitous, which is always problematic for the person in whom such a lack of character exists (James 1:8, Matthew 6:24). Waves of instability flood their lives resulting in lost jobs, lost possessions, lost families, and ultimately lost souls.

Integrity was what Job had. He knew what was important and even in dire circumstances, while under immense pressure, he stayed the course. Let us be such people, who regardless of the test, do not deviate from the course that was set for us before the foundation of the world. There is a reward for such people in this world and the one to come.

## RECOMMENDATIONS:

Determine what really matters to you.
Set your priorities and goals accordingly.
Don't deviate or compromise one iota.

*Journey Notes:*

# DAY 17 – THE JOURNEY
## IDENTITY CRISIS

*Memory Verse: Jeremiah 1:5*

*Before I formed thee in the belly I knew thee; and before thou camest forth out of the womb I sanctified thee, and I ordained thee a prophet unto the nations.*

**Today's Scripture Reading:** 1 Peter 2:4-11

The desire to be liked and accepted is among the greatest NEEDS we have as human beings. Rejection and isolation never feel good. This is why, even as children, both were used in small doses to help shape us socially. Being separated from the group and placed in timeout had an impact because we were excluded from the camaraderie and fun that others were experiencing. Invariably, there was someone in the group who went to great lengths to exaggerate the level of enjoyment they were having. Even though you knew exactly how it felt to slide down a sliding board, or climb the monkey bars, their apparent glee made your exclusion that much more painful.

As believers who are in this world, but not of it, there will be instances when we, as a matter of choice, separate ourselves from certain environments and activities because they don't glorify God. There will be other times that our difference in beliefs, and our unwillingness to compromise them, will cause others to separate themselves from us (John 15:19, Luke 6:22, 23). We are told in God's Word not to conform to this world (Romans 12:2). It may not FEEL good to be left out, laughed at, or even picked on because of your boldness in Christ, but it is and will be worth it (I Peter 4:1-5).

Your citizenship is in Heaven. As such, you are governed by different laws, rules, and ethics. There is a higher standard for you. You've been given the power of the Holy Ghost to equip you to live up to that standard (Philippians 3:12-21). You're CHOSEN, ROYALTY, CALLED, ORDAINED, KINGS, and PRIESTS (Revelation 1:6)! Who cares about the sliding boards and monkey bars of this life?! Life is about more than that! You've been translated from the kingdom of darkness into the Kingdom of His dear Son (Colossians 1:13)! Rejoice that you're counted worthy to suffer for His Name (2 Thessalonians 1:3-12, Acts 5:41)! God had a plan for your life before the foundation of the world. Ask Him to reveal it. Then, Live it out!

## RECOMMENDATIONS:

Evaluate whether or not you're suffering from an identity crisis.

### Here are some signs:
Willingness to compromise God-ordained principles in order to be included in cliques, groups, clubs, and organizations.
An unwillingness to speak out in mixed company (saved/lost) for righteousness, and against sin.
Bouts of depression, feelings of loneliness and isolation associated with your sanctification.
Living as close to the world as possible without going "over the line."

# DAY 18 – THE JOURNEY
## SHOW MERCY

*Memory Verse: Luke 6:36*

*Be ye therefore merciful, as your Father also is merciful.*

**Today's Scripture Reading:** I John 3:14-18

There are certain things in our Christian walk that we can receive, only after we've given them. Forgiveness is one of those; mercy is another. Mercy is not simply feeling sorry for someone, or having pity on them. It's literally deeper than that. The word mercy in the Greek translates to "active compassion." The term compassion is translated as movement that originates in the bowels of an individual. It is not a perfunctory exercise designed to alleviate feelings of sympathy, or assuage pangs of guilt. Showing mercy requires action that one feels compelled, driven, and called to accomplish.

On several occasions, Jesus was moved with compassion toward people (Matthew 9:36, 14:14, Mark 1:41). In each case, He DID something to exemplify His concern. Mercy doesn't say "somebody ought to do something!" It doesn't spout off high sounding soliloquies designed to feign concern. As a matter of fact, mercy doesn't SAY anything. Mercy MUST be shown!

In Matthew 18, when the man was forgiven of his debt, it was mercy that precipitated that forgiveness. The lord of the servant was moved with compassion. That's mercy! To be so touched by someone's pain, plight, and powerlessness that we are moved to intervene even to our own detriment. We have been, and continue to be, the recipients of mercy from God and from others (Lamentations 3:21-23)! We need it so let's be sure to show mercy (Matthew 5:7).

## RECOMMENDATIONS:

Evaluate your compassion response:
Are you aware of the problems of people around you?
Are you regularly moved to action when encountering the plight of others?
Are the resources under your stewardship available as a part of the solution?

*Journey Notes:*

# DAY 19 – THE JOURNEY
# FAITH

*Memory Verse: 2 Corinthians 5:7*

*For we walk by faith, not by sight:*

**Today's Scripture Reading:** Hebrews 11, John 19

For some years now, I've defined faith as the constant belief in what God says that serves as the barometer for EVERYTHING the believer does. It is our belief in the promises of God that causes them to be realized in our lives. Perhaps, like me, you read the Bible before you were born again and were unmoved by Its Words. They didn't produce life or stir you to action UNTIL you believed.

All great work is done by faith, and whatever is not motivated by belief does not please God (Romans 14:23, Hebrews 11:6). When we are attacked, it is our faith that Satan is trying (testing) (1 Peter 1:7). It all begins and ends with our faith. That's why Jesus is the author (initiator, originator) and the finisher (completer) of our faith (Hebrews 12:2). When Jesus comes in all of His glory, He is coming for those in whom there is this abiding faith (Luke 18:8). I've heard it said, and I agree, that the number one duty of the believer is TO BELIEVE!

This fact does not absolve us from our duty to act. Au Contraire, beloved! The belief of which I speak is not the heady, ethereal belief of intellectuals who live to pontificate endlessly and impress others with their extreme verbosity. No! This is that deep, visceral, indomitable faith that demands action. Like mercy, which is incubated in the same chamber of the soul, faith hurls us into action. Faith that does not do so, simply is not faith (James 2:14-20)! The faith that we have is THE SAME spirit of faith which our predecessors possessed (2 Corinthians 4:13, Romans 12:3). Miracles were wrought, lives were changed, and souls were saved all because they believed. They refused to compromise their beliefs even under the threat of death. Oh God, let such a faith be my anchor and rudder in times of storm.

## RECOMMENDATIONS:

Examine your faith.
Is what you believe, or believing for, based in the Scriptures?
Does your belief produce visible works?
Is your belief unwavering?

*Journey Notes:*

# DAY 20 – THE JOURNEY
## HOPE

*Memory Verse: Zechariah 9:12*

*Turn you to the strong hold, ye prisoners of hope: even to day do
I declare that I will render double unto thee.*

**Today's Scripture Reading:** Titus 2:1-13, John 20

Blessed assurance, Jesus is mine. Oh what a foretaste of glory divine. Heir of salvation, purchase of God. Born of His Spirit, washed in His blood. This is my story, this is my song, praising my Savior all the day long. I do remember this great hymn of the church well. As a young boy, it was one of my favorites. Assurance was scarce and a rare commodity in my life at the time. There was little, that was good, that I could rest in or be confident of. You can imagine how exhilarating it was for me to fathom that I could rest in the fact that Jesus, the King, Savior, and Messiah, was MINE! If this was possible, ANYTHING was possible. The hope in Christ became the foundation for all of my hopes and dreams. This is as it should be.

The hope of eternal life is the preeminent hope which serves as an anchor for the soul (Hebrews 6:17-19). Once this hope is settled, it prevents ambivalence. In addition to stability, this hope streamlines our lives because any hope or dream that doesn't fit this foundational hope is summarily dismissed. This keeps us from wasting precious time entertaining frivolous "opportunities," and pursuing distractions, disguised as blessings. Hope is one of the three elements of Christian character. Faith and love are the other two. This hope (trust, confidence, and assurance) is a living hope that is perennial, living throughout the year, year after year (1 Peter 1:3)!

Hope sees the invisible thing that faith believes for. It is this hope of the glory of God that causes us to rejoice before a thing materializes. Hope is the result of a sequential process of tribulation, patience, and experience that creates hope. No ingredient can be left out if hope is to be produced. No tribulation is pleasant, but we must exhibit patience in tribulation in order to gain the experience of coming through it (Romans 5:3). Hope looks both ways: forward in anticipation of what's coming and backward in gratitude for what has been done. Hope governs our thoughts, words, and actions, causing them to be positive and life forming. In many ways, we become prisoners of hope.

## RECOMMENDATIONS:

Become a prisoner of Hope.
Give God glory in tribulation.
Wait on the Lord for His deliverance instead of taking shortcuts out of trials.
Know that if God allowed it, it's for your good.

*Journey Notes:*

# DAY 21 – THE JOURNEY
# LOVE

*Memory Verse -1 John 4:7*

*Beloved, let us love one another: for love is of God; and every one that loveth is born of God, and knoweth God.*

**Today's Scripture Reading:** 1 Corinthians 13 and John 21

In keeping with the Kingdom principle of the last being first, the last lesson presented on our Journey is the most important of them all. Love is so important that it is the one characteristic by which God identifies Himself. Love is also the distinguishing characteristic by which the world identifies us as His disciples (John 13:35). The love of God, which indwells us as believers, is shed abroad in our hearts by the Holy Ghost. It is not relationship driven, nor is it concerned with itself (Luke 6:32, 1 Corinthians 13: 4-5).

As previously stated, faith, hope, and love are the three elements of Christian character. The greatest of these is love. The love of God is separated from other forms of love in that it is UNCONDITIONAL. Being filled with the Spirit equips us to love those who hate us, bless those who curse us, and pray for those who despitefully use us (Matthew 5:43-44; Luke 6:28). God's love is so amazing that the exhibition of it alone is enough to convince unbelievers of God's reality.

Faith works by love (Galatians 5:6). This fact provides clarity to the text "whatsoever is not of faith is sin" (Romans 14:23). Only what is motivated by love, is honored by God. What we do cannot bring glory to us or be born out of a competitive nature (Philippians 2:3). The Love of God is not something we work to possess. It is simply the result of the crucifixion of our flesh, combined with the acquisition of God's nature. It is the primary fruit of the Spirit (Galatians 5:22). As you continue your journey, remember to keep yourselves in the love of God (Jude 1:21).

## RECOMMENDATIONS:

Praise God for His Love.
Review your journal.

**Color code your entries:**
Rhema
Doctrine
Reproof/Correction
Instruction

Pray over your entries, Listen for God's voice, Obey.

*Journey Notes:*

# THE JOURNEY
## CONCLUSION

The gravitational pull of the Spirit of God is at work. As His people, we are being drawn into a place of deeper revelation, commitment, and fellowship. Make no mistake, as if you could, having taken The Journey, this is a God thing.

Yes, we are appreciative of the fact that we have been born again, washed in the blood, and translated from the kingdom of darkness, into the Kingdom of light. But there is a yearning, a craving, yea even a cry, from the depths of our being for MORE. We cry for more because this time has given us a glimpse into the boundless depths of our God. We are more cognizant of what is available and possible. Things that we thought unattainable three weeks ago are suddenly within reach.

Reach for them! Press toward the mark for the prize of the high calling of God, in Christ Jesus. Continue your Journey. As you do, may the Lord, Jesus, our great King, bless you with His unprecedented favor!

*Journey Notes:*

# ABOUT THE AUTHOR

Bishop Rick August is the Senior Pastor of Greater Grace Apostolic Assembly and the Presiding Prelate of the International Alliance of Apostolic Ministries. As early as the age of four years, though he could not comprehend it at the time, Bishop August knew he was called by God to preach His Word. At the age of 18, he acknowledged his call to ministry, preaching his first sermon at the age of 19, while serving in active duty in the United States Air Force.

Bishop August has served God faithfully in many capacities over his 30 plus years of being saved. Following the leadership of the Lord, Bishop August separated from the United States Air Force and in February 1990, with a total of 11 people, launched Greater Grace Apostolic Assembly in Biloxi, MS. As this ministry has grown, so has its commitment to global evangelism. This commitment places great demands on Bishop August nationally and internationally as a church growth seminar conductor, conference speaker, revivalist, and church planter. Bishop August has been instrumental in helping to launch several churches. In addition to those duties, moving on a mandate from God, Bishop August launched an organization, the International Alliance of Apostolic Ministries (I.A.A.M.), which provides a place of fellowship, training, and healing for Apostolic ministries around the world. I.A.A.M. has been established as a place of covering and fellowship for brethren whose hearts are set to "contend for the faith which was once delivered unto the saints."

Bishop August is married to Evangelist Tammi August and is the father of seven children and grandfather of four. He feels blessed to have his family serving with him in ministry at Greater Grace Apostolic Assembly.

Bishop Rick August has been described as a bold, innovative leader who is on the cutting edge culturally and philosophically. When asked to sum up his accomplishments thus far, he responds, "to God be the glory; great things He hath done."

For more information about Bishop Rick August
www.mygreatergrace.com

# THE JOURNEY

*Journey Notes:*

*Journey Notes:*

# THE JOURNEY

*Journey Notes:*

*Journey Notes:*